LUCK IS NOT A STRATEGY

A guide to planning, implementing, and boosting career success

SUZANNE RICCI

TABLE OF CONTENTS

Success is a word used in many aspects of our life. Success is a word we use to measure our career, our family, relationships, learning outcomes, business, happiness, and more. However, success is a subjective and highly personal concept. How a person measures success or the specific measurements we use varies from person to person and event to event. At least they should.

For the most part, we are raised to think that success is a single terminus. You reach it or you don't. In my experience, I have come to realize success in family, in career, in education, and in life are all defined in different ways. For example, my definition of career success and my definition of family success are separate and distinct. Granted they do overlap in some instances; however, my success as a mom has no impact on my career success and vice-versa. Technically, I could reach my success definition for motherhood and not ever achieve my defined career success.

This workbook was created to help individuals define and reach their desired career success. Although I get asked for help in other areas, I am not a counselor. I am just someone who has helped thousands curate their desired career journey and put them on their way to reaching their defined career success.

I have interviewed thousands of people from all different income levels, success levels, and educational backgrounds throughout my career. I have always asked them the same question: how do you measure success? I ask this question to see what is truly important to the person. Some say money, relationships, feeling good, accepting God, working out daily. I have heard all kinds of answers to the question, but rarely do I hear the same response from two or more people. I also rarely hear anyone say, "It depends on what we're talking about."

Why are the responses always different? Because success is defined differently by everyone and is largely influenced by a person's experiences throughout life. For example, my sister and I are incredibly close. We have been our entire life. We had the same upbringing, but different experiences—everything from travel to education—led to our drawing disparate conclusions. We have two very different definitions of career success—neither right nor wrong. Just our own definitions.

As you set out on your journey of mapping your career success, using this workbook, know that your definition of success is unique to you. You must be true to how you define success. I hope you will use this book to determine what is important to you, clarifying your definition of success and cultivating a career plan that meets your desired results. Don't let others influence your purpose. The only way to achieve success is to be true to what you want your career to be.

Your definition of success is what will motivate you to continue implementing, tweaking, and living your tiered success plan.

Also, remember that it's ok for your plans to change. This is normal, but try to create a definition that truly represents what you feel success is and then adjust as needed.

The more honest you are about how you define success, the more likely it is that you will create a plan that works.

That being said, congratulations on taking the first step in planning your future. It doesn't matter what stage you're at in your career. Your age and educational background don't matter either. After years of helping thousands of individuals reach their career goals, I created the tiered approach outlined in this workbook. I know the tiered system can help you get to where you want to go too.

A few words of advice to utilize this workbook successfully:

- Be honest with yourself.

- Reflect on your abilities and your desires.

- Understand that your plan can and should change.

- Never beat yourself up.

- Celebrate your wins for no less than twenty-four hours.

- Forget about your losses in less than twenty-four minutes.

- Although ignorance may be bliss, it is very dangerous.

- Do research. You don't know what you don't know. Research is the only way to learn and to make informed decisions.

- Reach out via email if you have any questions.

I am here to help. This is not a get-rich-quick plan. This workbook is designed to help you define your own level of career success and work on your career plan.

CHAPTER 1

THE EVOLUTION OF CAREER SUCCESS

In the 1950s, 1960s, and up to the early 1990s, staying put or maintaining company loyalty was the way to a successful career, per society's standards. It was well known that to make it up the corporate ladder, you needed to stay put at one company, learn the culture, be known as the best at whatever job you were doing, and make sure everyone liked you. Company politics played a crucial role in career success throughout this time. It was possible to make it pretty far in a company, if not all the way up the corporate ladder, starting at a company at age eighteen, with no outside work experience or education.

Today, you will be hard-pressed to find these same opportunities in the workforce. So, what is the modern secret to career success? How can you plan to be successful if loyalty no longer buys career success? First, let's look at what happened. What caused the change?

By the 1990s, a lot had changed in society and pop culture. These changes were affecting the workplace. Technology and computers were now widely accepted and seen in almost every office.

Generation X, the generation born roughly from the early 1960s to mid-1970s, often perceived to be disaffected and directionless, was coming out of high school and college. They were the first generation that had grown up with computers and the newly adopted widely spreading technologies found in the vast majority of workplaces.

Generation X had computers in grade, middle, and high school, and many had computers at their houses as well. The Internet was now readily available to the masses through dial-up technology, and AOL had made chatting with others from around the world a possibility. Generation X had so many changes happening in the world around them.

Being defined as "directionless," staying at one company was no longer a reality for this generation. They craved new experiences; they were risk-takers, not wanting the security their baby boomer parents needed and desired. Remember, this is the generation they invented *Head Bangers Ball for.* They wanted new things, new directions, and new technology. As a result, "job-hopping" became the new norm.

Something interesting happened through Generation X and the job-hopping scenarios . . . the Generation X employees were learning new skills at each company they moved to. They took the good and the bad and applied what they learned at the various companies they were hopping to and from.

Up to this point, staying employed at one company was the key to career success. However, through Generation X moving from one job to another, we learned that people are able to improve companies by applying different cultural mindsets or other things they learned along the way.

Also, technology jobs were trendy, and moving from one company to another became the way to make more money and upgrade your skills in the technology sector.

This brings us to today. As a result of Generation X and their inability to focus or stay put, job-hopping became the norm. It is now socially acceptable, and studies show a direct effect on career success from changing jobs. *Forbes* magazine did a survey, and on average, workers stay at their companies for 4.4 years.

Since job-hopping is now part of how we move up the ladder and how we can hit our desired career milestones, it is more important than ever to have a plan that makes sense for your career.

Caution: Changing jobs without purpose is still seen as taboo in the workplace and will hurt your career. Before we move on, let's be clear. I advocate changing jobs with a purpose, not hopping out of boredom or for any other nonsensical reason.

With this knowledge, I created the tiered approach to career success. Using the tiered approach to success, you should include multiple career moves that all have a purpose in your plan. Over the years, the clients I have worked hardest for were those who showed up at my office after being unexpectedly laid off from a company they had stayed with for 15+ years. No warnings, no thank you. Just goodbye. They were often the hardest hit emotionally and had to work the hardest to get their careers back on track.

You're probably wondering why it was so hard if they had been at one company for so long. The answer is because other companies now saw these professionals as one-sided, not dimensional enough. They were now perceived as "slackers." Other companies believed that they were never willing to invest in themselves because they didn't have to; they only wanted job security, and they were resistant to change, possessing antiquated skills and minimal networks. Therefore, they were unwanted.

What a change in perception!

Understandably, when writing your plan today, if you are employed, you may not know what companies to move to by name. You may not even know the name of the desired department within your same company if you choose to stay put (but move up). The plan doesn't need to include that level of detail, just the timeframe for moving and a reason for the move. That reason can be more money, a new job title, different responsibilities, added skills, etc.

For example, if you were interested in being a project manager and your long-term goal was to make $100,000/year, you would want to take the tiered approach to achieve this overall goal. You would start as an Associate Project Manager or Project Coordinator—tier one. You would need to write out the skills you want to obtain, project types you would like to work on, volunteer projects, etc.—everything that would enable you to move up to project manager—tier two. Then, you could have the goal to be a senior project manager, making more than $100,000 annually within five years. Within each step, you will write out the skills required, the certifications and continued education you will need to plan for, the types of projects or budgets you will want to manage, and the desired companies or industries you want to work in.

Crucial to success planning is writing your career statement or career goal. To enable you to meet your goals, you will want to use the SMART Goal writing techniques at each level. To make your career statements SMART, ensure they are:

- Specific

- Measurable

- Attainable

- Relevant

- Time-Based.

An example of a career goal for the above Project Manager might look something like this: By year three, I want to manage projects with a total budget of 20% more than my current job, working within the solar/sustainability industries. I will target jobs that have salaries of *$65,000–80,000/year.* Let's break down this goal to ensure it is SMART.

Specific – The goal has a particular job title and salary range desired.

Measurable – The goal is measurable because you will determine if you are making this move within three years and obtaining a new salary.

Attainable – This goal is possible if you are currently a project coordinator and working on the projects and skills you need to move up to project manager. This goal will not be achievable if you are unwilling to invest in new skills or continue your project management skills.

Realistic – This goal is practical because it falls within the range of what project managers with three years of experience make. Depending on where you live, you want to be sure your current job market supports your goal.

Time-Based – This goal is timely because it says within three years. We can mark a date on the calendar and set milestones to achieve this goal on the way.

In the next chapter, we will explore the Tiered Approach to Career Planning and start writing out our plan.

CHAPTER 2

THE TIERED APPROACH TO CAREER PLANNING

Throughout our childhood, we inevitably hear something along the lines of "Grow Up and Become Successful," "Study Hard and You Will Succeed," or "Make Smart Choices." The truth is that very few people get the guidance they need to learn *how* to become successful, study hard, or make smart choices.

Think about it. Did anyone ever help you define success? We use the words "become successful" all the time. We see it in school advertisements, articles in magazines, and on the covers of books, but what definition of success is being used? Or I should say *whose* definition of success is being used? The definition of success is different for every person. The definition of success also changes depending on the stage in life you are at.

What about teaching you how to study? In school, you were probably told to "study hard," but did anyone ever teach you study techniques? We even have "study hall," but rarely are we taught study strategies. And when is the last time someone taught you how to make a smart choice? Many people learn these things through the school of hard knocks by watching others. I have acquired most of my knowledge from reading countless books and mentors. Sometimes, we just "keep trying" because that is all we know how to do. However, most of the time, we have no real concept of what we are doing. Only a lucky few have stumbled upon useful guidance.

LET'S GET INTO PLANNING

Over the years, I noticed the difference between people who could achieve success and people who just couldn't make it happen. Many were ordinary people with the same education, living situation, and opportunities—seemingly equal in just about every way. So, what was the difference? To sum it up, the successful ones knew two things. First, they knew how to start. (I will share the necessary steps to getting started on reaching your path to career success with you.) Second, they had a realistic definition of what I call "tiered success." Basically, this means that your definition of success has to change over time. If your definition of success *doesn't* change over time, you will either burn out and never reach your goal or, worse, you will start to move backward due to a feeling of defeat.

My very first customer used the tiered approach to reach his ultimate career goal. He was a retired military professional who went back to school to get a bachelor's degree in information technology (IT); he had been laid off from a service company and decided to move to a new area. He took advantage of his layoff and decided it was the time to change careers. He had no formal IT experience; he was just what we call a "home hobbyist" with a degree. Together, we came up with a realistic tiered plan for success. First, he started off making less than what he eventually wanted to make. He continued to work on his plan annually, being sure to change his definition of success as he went until he was finally earning the amount of money he had desired within the industry. It didn't happen overnight; he put in a lot of hard work. But he did reach his final career success goal because he had realistic definitions of success along the way and used the tiered approach until he achieved the level of career success he wanted.

One of the advantages of the tiered approach is you have time to figure out what tactics and strategies are needed along the way, depending on the situation you are in at any given moment. By not taking advantage of the time that a tiered approach affords, you may find yourself setting unrealistic goals, like the truck driver who called me once about a course I was teaching. Upon completion of my course, the average salary of participants was $70,000 a year, but most of the graduates had the experience. This program was a professional development course. Not a beginner course. When I explained it was unrealistic to start in this industry with no experience at making $70,000 a year, he hung up on me. He had an unrealistic definition of success and wasn't willing to apply the tiered approach to reach his goals.

STEP 1: DO YOUR RESEARCH

If you are new to an industry, changing careers, or just starting your first career, you may not know what is truly realistic or where to start. I suggest starting with online research. Just be sure you are using valid and reliable resources. It's important to differentiate between someone's biased opinion and facts. A reliable starting point for valuable career path information is the industry association in your field. The Department of Labor and your local workforce center will also have information to point you in the right direction.

Next, interview people within your desired industry. Don't just interview the person in the ultimate position you want. Interview people in all the jobs you will need to hold to obtain your ultimate position. Learn from their experiences. Using social media, LinkedIn, and your own personal and professional networks, you will be surprised how many connections you can make with people who will take the time to speak with you and share any information they have, including their career successes and failures.

Remember, you can sometimes learn more from failure than from success.

When interviewing people, be sure you are considerate of their time. Interviews can be scheduled via online chat, services such as Skype, traditional phone, email, or in-person. Always keep your talk to the amount of time they agreed to. Have a list of pre-planned and printed questions and take notes quickly, so you can get a lot covered. Ask about their education, career path, what they would have done differently, and their suggestions for getting into a position like theirs. Keep in mind that times change. Depending on how long they've had their job, the path to that position may be very different now. Don't forget to ask about this.

During the interview, be sure to ask about their daily tasks. Think about if those daily tasks interest you. I have had several clients come to meet with me, telling me they want to do a particular job, but when I ask them what tasks a person in that job does, they are way off. I have had several clients over the years who have in-demand medical credentials. When I ask them why they don't want to work in the medical field, I hear things like, "I don't like blood," or "I am very introverted, and I don't want to work with people." If they had done the step-two research phase, they would have uncovered that this was not a realistic career path for them. It would have saved them time and money.

If you receive conflicting information from your research, I suggest you look at why you received conflicting reports. Do the interviewees have up-to-date information? Are they out of touch with their industry? Was one of them being nice and trying to sugar-coat the path to success? Ultimately, your research from associations, the Department of Labor, and your local workforces should help you get a clear picture.

SAMPLE QUESTIONS TO ASK IN CAREER RESEARCH INTERVIEWS

- What type of education do you recommend to obtain this career?

- What type of skills, not taught in a degree, do you recommend?

- What are the tasks you perform throughout the day?

- What is the most important skill you use in your job?

- What do you like most about your position?

- What do you like least about your position?

These are just samples. Try to come up with more questions on your own that are relevant to your career path.

BREAKING IT DOWN AND PUTTING IT ON PAPER

Defining career success begins with breaking down your ultimate goal into smaller goals. Achieving smaller goals is always more manageable, and you tend to stay motivated because you are achieving things and experiencing wins along the way. Start with clear, concise, and realistic career goals, and then move on to strategies and tactics to help you achieve them. If your ultimate goal is to make $80,000 a year, be sure you are realistic. Your industry must present that opportunity, you must have a clear career path, and you must be willing to invest in the education and skills training required to get to that level. Also, be realistic about whether you are willing to work the hours and do the tasks required. Most often, making more than $50,000 a year comes with longer work hours and harder work. If you know you want to spend ample time with friends and family and work forty hours per week, then make a realistic plan that accommodates this definition of success. I once had a customer move from New England to Tampa, Florida. He wanted to make the same salary for the same job in Tampa as he did in New England. This isn't realistic, so he ultimately didn't achieve his first definition of success. We worked together to develop a clear, concise, and realistic career goal for his current situation, which I am happy to say he achieved.

Once you feel comfortable with the path and the skills you will need, it's critical to put your plan on paper. Remember, the plan can change, and it will need to change, but having it written down will make it easier for you to take the first step. Depending on where you are in your career, you can write out one-year, three-year, and five-year goals. If you are new to your career, then write out seven- and ten-year goals too. Your written goals should include approximate salaries and approximate job titles. If you know the company you would like to work for, write that down also. The more detailed the written plan is, the easier it will be to execute it.

SKILLS AND EDUCATION

Now that we have talked about a written plan of where you want to be, it is time to be realistic about what it will take to get you there. Make a list of the skills you have today and the skills you will need to achieve at each milestone. Remember, you should be gathering abilities along the way. For example, your seven-year plan should list all the skills you need to acquire to reach your seven-year goal. You're probably not going to have every skill or credential you need at the beginning. That's okay. Even if you have a college degree, you most likely will be missing some hard or soft skills required or desired for the field you've chosen. Education and training are usually a significant part of achieving career success.

You may need specific skills that aren't taught in high school or college to accomplish a specific task. Acquiring additional skills doesn't mean you need another degree, a new degree, or any degree at all. Continuing education or training may be the missing link for you. Get all the information you need to decide on the training classes, seminars, workshops, conferences, and educational opportunities that will allow you to obtain the skills you need for the opportunities outlined in your plan. Be sure the skills are in line with the research you have gathered and are necessary to take the next step.

If you determine that you need additional education, taking the time to do further research when selecting a school is vital. Don't rely on the recommendation of a friend or family member. They may have different needs than you concerning education. This choice is important for reaching your goals. Go and visit all the schools, training centers, and seminar facilities in your area that teach the skills you seek. Take a list of questions to ask when you're meeting with the school representative(s). School representatives should be familiar with the job opportunities you're pursuing and have some information about how the skills they teach will help you achieve your goals. You should never be asked to sign up on the same day unless the class starts that day. Take the information you gathered home, think about it, compare your options, and make an informed decision.

SAMPLE QUESTIONS TO ASK EDUCATIONAL FACILITIES

- What format does this program run? Is it self-paced, online, hybrid, etc.

- Is this school licensed?

- Does this school need to be accredited for this particular program?

- Do the instructors have industry experience?

- Does this program cover all costs? Books, certification, exams, retakes, etc.

- Do I have to take a test to earn the certification? If so, where is the exam and when?

- Are there job placement services available? What is the success rate?

- Does this school participate in the community?

If you have trouble making a choice, I suggest going with the school that seemed more knowledgeable in your field or will let you sit in on a class before signing up. Education is a significant decision, and you shouldn't feel pressured. And finally, remember to reinvest in learning new skills every year, even if you are at the level of success you desire. Obtaining new skills every year will help you reach or keep you at your defined level of success.

CAREER PLANNING ACTIVITIES

I would like to make a career plan for:

__ 1 year   __ 3 years   __ 5 years   __ longer

LIST 5 CHARACTERISTICS OF CAREER SUCCESS FOR YOU:

1.

2.

3.

4.

5.

What job title do you ultimately want to have?

_____

What industry do you want to work in?

_____

What type of education do you need to achieve your goals?

_____

Do you want to pursue self-employment?

_____

How many hours per week are you willing and able to work without sacrificing your happiness?

_____

What are your current strengths as they relate to your career?

_____

What are your current weaknesses as they relate to your career?

_____

What opportunities are there in your desired career path?

_____

What threats are there in your desired career path?

_____

Can you convert any of your weaknesses to strengths?

_____

What should you avoid in your career path?

_____

SWOT ANALYSIS

Strengths

1.
2.
3.
4.
5.
6.
7.

Weaknesses

1.
2.
3.
4.
5.
6.
7.

Opportunities

1.
2.
3.
4.
5.
6.
7.

Threats

1.
2.
3.
4.
5.
6.
7.

Using the answers on the previous page, write out your ultimate career goal.

My ultimate career goal is:

_____

My ultimate career goal is SMART: (make sure all are checked)

☐ Specific   ☐ Measurable   ☐ Attainable   ☐ Realistic   ☐ Timely

What are the names of jobs or career positions in between where you are now and your ultimate career goal?

_____

Tip: Use Google to find alternative job titles for the same role.

Using the ultimate career position and the positions between now and your top position, create career goals for the years between now and your ultimate career goal.

One-Year Career Goal:

_____

Three-Year Career Goal:

_____

Five-Year Career Goal:

_____

Year 5

Year 4

Year 3

Year 2

Year 1

What skills will you need to obtain between now and year three to be successful in landing the types of jobs you desire?

_____

What education or training will you need to be successful in meeting your year three career goal? Remember hard and soft skills.

_____

What certifications or credentials can you acquire that will make you stand out and help you achieve your goals?

_____

What skills will you need to obtain between now and year five to be successful in landing the types of jobs you desire?

_____

What education or training will you need to be successful in meeting your year five career goal? Remember hard and soft skills.

_____

What certifications or credentials can you acquire that will make you stand out and help you achieve your goals?

_____

CHAPTER 3

PERSONAL BRANDING FOR CAREER SUCCESS

As defined by Wikipedia, personal branding is "the conscious and intentional effort to create and influence public perception of an individual by positioning them as an authority in their industry, elevating their credibility, and differentiating themselves from the competition, to ultimately advance their career, increase their circle of influence, and have a larger impact."

Personal branding goes hand in hand with responsibility. We are responsible for the image and perception we give people about ourselves.

Personal branding isn't just about what we wear, although how you present yourself is a part of branding; personal branding is a complete package that tells the world we are. In career success, the brand we display will play an important part in reaching our career goals.

Creating a winning personal brand can lead to:

- Improved career prospects

- Better contacts and clients

- Industry recognition

SOME ASPECTS OF PERSONAL BRANDING INCLUDE:

- Appearance

- Grammar/choice of words

- Upholding your commitments

- Accountability for your actions

- Publicity

- Volunteering (at work and in non-profits)

This section of the workbook will help you create a vision for your brand and help you create your blueprint for building your brand. Remember, brand building never stops! As simple as the term "branding" may sound, it plays a role in determining your career success. This is because an outstanding reputation can help you overcome several obstacles and allow you to forge ahead in your chosen career.

Jeff Bezos defined branding as "what someone says about you when you are not in the room." For your career, this statement is powerful. Would your colleagues suggest you for a project if you weren't in the room, or would they say you aren't a good fit?

Curating a solid brand and an outstanding reputation is a choice. Luckily, we can start engaging in techniques to stand out and achieve the career milestones we set.

Tip: Make a list of at least five thought-leaders in your field that you aspire to be like, and follow them on the various social media platforms. Research everything about them, including what makes them different, how they got to where they are, where they contribute their thinking, etc. Success leaves trails, and you can rise to the top if you take inventory of who's already there.

The concept of branding for career success is about creating and crafting a perfect blend of your accomplishments, skills, values, and experiences, then presenting these items in various ways to the public.

Branding allows you to cultivate what people perceive about you. Branding helps an organization identify the value you could add. It also determines the types of roles and companies that are a good match for your talent and core values.

Although developing a personal brand for career success might sound challenging, there are some effective techniques you can start employing on a daily basis. By implementing branding techniques daily, you will experience a compounding effect in no time.

DEFINING YOUR BRAND

Implementing your brand all starts with defining what your brand is. To begin defining your brand, think about the words you want people to say about you when you are not around.

Examples of words that come to mind are: valuable, creative, consistent, thoughtful, brilliant, innovative, and helpful. These words are essential because we will use them when we develop our content plan later on.

ACTIVITIES

Write down a list of at least ten words you want to be associated with that describe you.

1.

2.

3.

4.

5.

6.

7.

8.

9.

10.

Now, ask four people you value to list at least ten words that describe you. Ask both professional colleagues and close friends or family. By diversifying who you ask, you will get a robust list and differing opinions.

1.

2.

3.

4.

5.

6.

7.

8.

9.

10.

Combine all of the lists. You should have at least fifty words now. Notice if any words repeat. Which words repeat the most? From this list of fifty, pick the ten words that resonate most with you.

1.

2.

3.

4.

5.

6.

7.

8.

9.

10.

Now that we have inspiration words for our brand, let's define what I call our "passion pillars." This step will help you identify what is important to you as a professional, what you want to be known for, and what drives you. Passion pillars are what your brand will be built upon, and your list of brand words may help you create three to four statements if you feel stuck. When writing out passion pillars, I like to finish the following sentence. "I am passionate about . . ."

Sample passion pillar statements.

- I am passionate about career success: mine and others.

- I am passionate about helping others achieve their defined career success.

- I am passionate about sustainable energy.

- I am passionate about helping reduce corporate carbon footprints by increasing recycling.

- I am passionate about emerging technology.

- I am passionate about my local community.

ACTIVITY

What do you enjoy doing most in your career?

_____

Are there industries you like or are fascinated with?

_____

Finish the following statements.

I am passionate about . . .

I am passionate about . . .

I am passionate about . . .

I am passionate about . . .

Now that you have your list of brand words and your passion pillars, you can create a branding statement. A branding statement consists of 1–2 sentences that accurately sum up what you do and what you stand for. Your brand statement is an effective way to sell yourself and your skills. You've probably heard of the thirty-second elevator pitch, but have you heard of the five-second elevator pitch? The five-second elevator pitch is suitable for use on your social media profiles, especially LinkedIn. Don't forget to incorporate the brand words you want to be associated with into the pitches. A convincing pitch will give people an idea of what you can do and why they should network with you.

Think of it as your unique selling proposition or your slogan. You can make it catchy, memorable, and attention-grabbing if you'd like. You can use your passion pillars to create one branding statement.

My branding statement is: I create customized training plans and innovative job search strategies to help IT and business professionals in Tampa Bay move toward their defined career success.

I can now use this branding statement to introduce myself at networking events or influence the branding techniques I use to ensure I stay on my defined brand.

DETERMINING YOUR GOALS

Next, we will move on to defining our goal(s). We start by asking ourselves, "What do you want to get out of branding?" Do you want to be an SME, start a side-hustle, land more job opportunities, become an author, or be known within your organization? You can define many different goals, but you will create a branding plan that allows you to reach your goal by defining a purpose.

ACTIVITY

What is (are) your branding goal(s)?

_____

Examples:

- **I want to be known as a subject matter expert in baking gluten-free pastries.**

- **I want to be known as a go-to person for fitness advice.**

- **I want to increase my sales by 50% through referrals.**

- **I want to earn $10,000 per year from Instagram.**

Tip: Use the SMART Technique to writing your branding goals we discussed in the previous chapter.

DEFINING YOUR TARGET MARKET

Next, we need to outline your target market. Defining your target market will help us reach the right people and ensure we are using the right platforms or methods to reach our market.

We can create a more effective branding plan if we know who we want to target. Generally, we can start to define our target market by thinking about who will be interested in what we have to say. An example would be individuals who work in sustainable energy or want to be physically fit. Often target markets have similar demographics or psychographics.

ACTIVITY

Who is your target market?

_____

CRAFTING OUR PLAN

Crafting the plan, you use for branding should be more accessible now that we know our goal and target market. Start by researching and thinking about how you can reach your target market.

ACTIVITY

What social media platforms does your target market use?

_____

What types of events does your target market attend?

_____

What types of educational content does your target market want to learn?

_____

Now that we know what social media platforms, what types of events, and what educational content our target market uses and wants, we can create content.

There are no right or wrong techniques for branding. Creating a plan that combines several techniques has worked well for me. It would be best if you found what works for you and what you are comfortable with. I have curated a list of several different ideas you can use for branding.

- Create social media posts on platforms that will reach your target market. For example, I use LinkedIn primarily, but a different platform like Instagram may be a better fit for other industries. Use the media that your target market uses.

Tip: You can use graphic creation software like Canva or Venngage to easily create compelling social media graphics that convey your brand. Remember to use your inspiration words to help. (We will cover using LinkedIn specifically in a separate section.)

- Share relevant content from reliable sources.

- Write content-specific articles to disseminate as blog posts or guest blog posts.

- Speak on relevant topics at conferences, workshops, or volunteer groups like Rotary or MeetUp.

Tip: To find speaking opportunities, you generally apply or ask for them. Conferences put out a "Call for Speakers." A Google search of Call for Speakers in your area or your industry should return a few good results. You can start to read the requirements and then apply. (I don't pay to speak. I look for free opportunities.)

- Host virtual webinars on your topic of choice. Sign up for a free Zoom account and post your webinar on Eventbrite. Then take a few screenshots while at the event and share them on your social.

- Launch a website or brand page on your social media platform.

CREATING YOUR CONTENT CALENDAR

Now that we have discussed various techniques you can use to disseminate your brand, you may want to create a content calendar to control what information you put out and when it gets released.

A content calendar allows us to determine when, where, and how we put out specific content. When crafting your content calendar, think about how many times you want to put content out. I like to create a regular schedule for branding. Having a regular schedule helps me stay organized and not get overwhelmed. I generally determine what I want my exposure to be each week based on what is going on. For example, I will create a plan to engage in ten branding pieces per week or five branding pieces per week based on my needs. Create a plan that works for you.

Tip: It is better to start with less branding and work up to more so you don't get overwhelmed. Once you are comfortable putting content out, it will be easier to add more content.

A sample weekly branding plan for me will look like the below:

Weekly Topic: Virtual networking success

Monday: Social post on LI, FB, IG, and Twitter: #motivationalmonday

Tuesday: Webinar: virtual networking success

Tuesday: Social post on LI and Twitter: #VirtualNetworkingSuccess

Wednesday: Guest speaking

Wednesday: LI post on #WinsDay

Wednesday: Networking event (I am attending)

Thursday: Virtual networking article released

Friday: Social post on LI, FB, IG, and Twitter: #funnyfriday

Friday: Virtual happy hour networking event (I am attending)

Saturday: Vertical video tip on virtual networking success

The above plan is a 17X content week for me. Why? Because I have 17 activities that are all brand building for me going on throughout the week. You can automate a lot of your posts using Hootsuite, Social Sprout, or Canva. I also use Sunday to plan my week of branding activities. Some weeks will only be 5X weeks. Some will be 20X weeks. Create a plan that makes you feel comfortable.

CONCLUSION

Career branding is not a once-and-done action but a process that produces the desired results over time. Start working on your career brand now, and continue working on it daily. You won't regret it.

SAMPLE ARTICLES HEADLINES

3 Tips To _____

4 Ways to _____

5 Key Takeaways from _____

6 Techniques to Transform Your _____

7 Things to Know Before _____

8 Tactics to _____

9 Things I Wished I'd Known Before _____

Top 10 _____ in the _____ Industry

SAMPLE WEEKLY CONTENT IDEAS WORKSHEET

Content (text going with visual)

Monday

Platform

Visual

Content (text going with visual)

Monday

Platform

Visual

Content (text going with visual)

Monday

Platform

Visual

Content (text going with visual)

Monday

Platform

Visual

Content (text going with visual)

Friday

Platform

Visual

Content (text going with visual)

Saturday

Platform

Visual

Content (text going with visual)

Sunday

Platform

Visual

ACTIVITIES

Do you have a Twitter account (handle)?

_____

Does your Twitter account provide a professional image of yourself?

_____

Are there any tweets you should delete?

_____

Conduct a general Twitter search for your career. What type of results and information did you receive?

_____

_____

_____

_____

_____

_____

Do you have a Linked In account? If yes, how complete is the profile?

_____

_____

_____

Can you improve the profile more?

_____

_____

_____

Is your Linked In Profile picture professional? Can you add a more professional photo?

_____

_____

_____

Search for and connect with a national association or local association that is geared toward your industry of choice.

_____

_____

_____

Sign up for volunteer opportunities

_____

_____

_____

Join one non-profit organization (e.g., Rotary, Junior Achievement, PPA)

_____

_____

_____

CHAPTER 4

PROFESSIONAL NETWORKING

We often hear that "networking is important to career success," but what is networking? It's essential to understand what networking is and isn't.

There are several misunderstandings when it comes to networking. It isn't about making fake friends or socializing with beer and wine on a nightly basis.

According to *Entrepreneur,* networking is the process of "Developing and using contacts made in business for purposes beyond the reason for the initial contact. For example, a sales representative may ask a customer for names of others who may be interested in his product." Although this definition is about making contacts in business, it is important to remember that networking is going on all around us. Often, we overlook experiences that allow us to expand our network in our daily lives. When I am out at my son's sports events, I am networking with the other parents, the coaches, the other team representatives. There are several ways to grow a network—some passive, some active—which we will explore below.

Now that we have a definition we can agree on, let's look at why networking is essential and how it can be done. The ability to network successfully can impact your career positively.

Networking gives us the ability to make contacts that we would never otherwise meet, get to know, or learn about new opportunities from. The goal for networking should be to build trusted relationships. Building trusted relationships means you are helping those you meet and they are helping you if needed.

Think about the people you currently know. Do you have that one friend who is excellent at meeting new people and good at staying in touch? Or, the friend who seems to always get fantastic job offers without applying? Or maybe the colleague that gets excellent referrals? There are two traits that make good networkers. Both of which we can learn and develop. The first is being able to talk to people. The second is following up. If you aren't an outgoing person or naturally social, this could sound scary, but there is good news. It's ok; you can learn to network successfully. You can learn to make small talk, and we have tools we can use to follow up.

TYPES OF NETWORKING

I break networking down into two categories. Active networking is when I am attending events and actively looking to meet people and grow my network. Active networking is done in face-to-face events or through virtual events. Passive networking is when I use social media or connection media to grow my network and strengthen my relationships through some of the branding techniques we discussed in the previous chapter. I like to use a combination of both types of networking. Depending on your goals and reasons for networking, you may want to engage in Active or Passive networking. However you choose to network, it is essential to remember you should never do networking with an insincere or phony approach.

NETWORKING DOS AND DON'Ts

When it comes to networking, you should avoid:

- Phoniness or insincerity.

- Events that don't fit your personality.

- Dance clubs.

- Drinking more than one alcoholic beverage while at events.

- Talking negatively about other people or businesses.

- Running out of business cards.

- Spending too much time talking to people you already know.

Remember, the purpose of networking is to make new contacts and to further other relationships by moving your relationships toward a higher level of trust.

When it comes to networking, you should:

- Find events that match your personality.

- Do research on the events and attendee list before attending.

- Have a plan for each event.

- Reach out to the event coordinator and introduce yourself. They usually know people at the event and can introduce you, which can make it easier to meet people

- Be a resource for others, and always have something to offer, be it a website, reference, connection, company, etc.

- Follow up with a kind note/email, and add the contact to a system that will allow you to follow up regularly.

- If you make a connection you have a genuine interest in or things in common with, follow-up and ask for a meeting to explore the possibilities of sharing resources.

CHATTING & SMALL TALK

Regardless if an event is face-to-face or virtual, you will need to talk to people if you want to grow your network. I consider myself outgoing and genuinely interested in others. I recognize not everyone is comfortable talking to strangers. With this in mind, I have a few tips.

- Pick events with topics that are of interest to you.

- Stay up to date with current events in business and pop culture.

- Sign up for newsletters from associations or organizations that disseminate the information you're interested in. For example, I receive several newsletters every morning in my inbox. These range from IT and HR industry associations like CompTIA and SHRM to national business magazines like *Forbes,* and I enjoy reading the local business journals' daily emails concerning what is going on in my local community.

- Avoid discussing anything controversial like religion or politics.

- Make a plan before each event, laying out a few talking topics and practicing them.

- Start a reading ritual. Reading a book per month will also help you have topics to talk about.

- Become familiar with the "Dale Carnegie Conversation Stack." Memorizing this stack and being comfortable with it has allowed me to engage in countless conversations with ease. You can google it, watch a YouTube video, or learn about it in a class provided by Dale Carnegie.

- Try to attend the same event multiple times, if it is possible. This will help you to strengthen relationships and meet numerous people.

- If you like an organization or event, get involved in the operation of the event if possible.

Tip: Remember, if someone doesn't engage with you or a conversation doesn't seem natural or hard to keep going, it isn't personal. I always remind myself to Q-Tip: Quit Taking it Personally. Tip: I tell my kids if friends aren't nice, find new friends. This applies to professional networking also.

ACTIVITY

- Research and sign up for at least five news-based newsletters, so you can start receiving industry information and local information to have talking points.

- Google "Dale Carnegie Conversation Stack," and become familiar with the points of creating small talk.

- Answer the below questions, so you'll be ready when asked in real life.

    o   Where are you from?

    _____

    o   What do you like about your hometown?

    _____

    o   What are your hobbies?

    _____

    o   I have traveled?

    _____

    o   What is a fun fact about you?

    _____

FOLLOWING UP

I know this may seem basic, but this is a step most people will miss. And there are some tactics I have found that make the process easier.

After each event, schedule time to follow up with anyone you meet. It can be the same day or the next day. When I book a networking event, I automatically schedule my follow-up time for that event. This way, I don't forget to schedule the follow-up or, worse, fail to follow up. If you receive business cards before leaving the event, consider writing what you learned about that person while in your car. It's what I do, and this activity helps me remember what we discussed or what to write about in my follow-up.

A follow-up can be via phone, text, or email. I decide how to follow up based on the conversations we had at the event. Sometimes I am comfortable calling others, but an email usually seems more appropriate for me.

FINDING NETWORKING EVENTS

Finding suitable networking events is essential. Nobody likes the feeling of wasting their time or meeting people you don't have much in common with. Nowadays, there are a few ways to find events.

Local industry associations, chambers of commerce, or other membership organizations will usually have events. These types of networking events are often in person or online. Generally, they are topic-driven and will allow you to meet individuals interested in those topics.

National associations, conferences, and seminars on topics of interest to you are other ways to expand your network and meet like-minded individuals. I recommend attending at least one national conference per year and a seminar or workshop at least twice a year, if not more.

Meetup.com is another resource for finding networking events in your local area. Meetup is a platform for finding and building local communities. People use Meetup to meet new people, learn new things, find support, get out of their comfort zones, and pursue their passions together. Meetup is built on the premise of helping individuals interested in the same topics get together in person, but some events are also online. Not all meetups are business-oriented. There are meetups for outdoor activities, photography, cooking, and more. Although most of the Meetups are free, some do charge. On Meetup, you can search for topics that interest you within a customizable radius of your zip code. Also, meetups are generally ongoing. Members may meet one time per month or week. Attending consistently allows you to grow relationships with people you meet and get to know them better.

You can also consider starting a Meetup if you like arranging events for others. This technique is a great way to expand your network rapidly, as you will have people coming to you.

Tip: Make sure you flesh out a complete profile on Meetup.com

Tip: When going to a meetup, I like to look at who else is signed up to attend. I read the profiles, so I know a little about the people who will be there.

Eventbrite.com is another resource for finding networking events. Generally, one-time events are posted on Eventbrite. You can search for local in-person events or online events.

ACTIVITIES

How many networking events do you want to attend per week?

Create a complete profile on Meetup.com.

Write down five areas you are interested in meeting like-minded individuals that can help you expand your network (e.g., photography, outdoor activities, women who code, career success, WordPress).

1.

2.

3.

4.

5.

Search Meetup for these five Meetup groups and join any Meetups that are interesting to you. (Note: Joining Meetup allows you to be notified if they post an event. It does not commit you to anything further.)

How many Meetups did you join?

Register and create a complete profile on Eventbrite.

Search for events in your area that are of interest to you.

How many events did you find?

Find your local associations and check their websites for events.

Create a networking calendar for the rest of the current month and next month.

STANDING OUT AT NETWORKING EVENTS

Statistically, most people find career opportunities through networking and the "hidden job market." Networking is one of the keys to career success. I have three rules to stand out at a face-to-face event.

1. Show up dressed to impress. Don't go overboard, but do dress one level above the expected dress code.

2. If you have the opportunity to speak, be sure to stand up. Even if nobody else stands up, you always should.

3. Always ask a question. If you know the topic ahead of time, you can research questions or ask friends and colleagues if they have any questions. Write them down and bring them with you.

As I write this, we are still being encouraged to have safer at-home practices, and virtual events are everywhere. I have adapted my three rules for the virtual world too.

1. Keep your camera on the entire time.

2. Show up dressed to impress. Don't go overboard, but dress one level above the expected dress code, even if it's from the waist up.

3. Always ask a question. If you know the topic ahead of time, you can research questions or ask friends and colleagues if they have any questions. Write them down and bring them with you.

Implementing the three rules to networking success will help you stand out and develop more substantial networks.

CHAPTER 5

FINDING CAREER SUCCESS USING LINKEDIN

LinkedIn is a professional social media platform. With more than 660 million members in its database at the time of writing, it is essentially a giant online Rolodex—on steroids. It's vital as professionals to maximize the chances of our profiles being found in relevant search queries. Like Google or any other search engine, LinkedIn uses a search algorithm to serve up results based on what the searcher is looking for. A well-optimized profile can lead to career success.

It's important to note there are different versions of LinkedIn. One is what I call Public LinkedIn—what you and I are (hopefully) using on a daily basis. Another is called LinkedIn Recruiter. LinkedIn Recruiter is one of LinkedIn's primary revenue streams and is used by recruiters to source candidates. 75 – 84% of recruiters use LinkedIn to source candidates. If your profile is not set up correctly, it will not be found in searches conducted on either the public or recruiter platform. It's that simple. When it comes to career success, being found in either version of LinkedIn can help you successfully implement your career success plan.

I often think of it like this: if we were in person, your LinkedIn profile is the equivalent of your appearance and how you behave in public. You wouldn't go out of your house half-dressed. And it would be best if you didn't keep a half-complete profile on LinkedIn.

At the time of writing, LinkedIn has five levels of profile strength. These levels include Beginner, Intermediate, Advanced, Expert, and All-Star. To achieve All-Star profile status, you need a:

1. **Profile Picture**
2. **Experience – Current and two prior positions**
3. **Skills – at least 5**
4. **Summary**
5. **Industry & Location**
6. **Education**
7. **Connections – at least 50**

PROFILE PICTURE

Having a professional profile picture on LinkedIn is a must. You will want to pick a color image that looks like you. It should be a high-resolution image, and your face should take up 60% of the picture. Always be the only person in the photo, and avoid the quick-fix temptation of a selfie at all costs.

Avoid using filters and distracting backgrounds. When selecting a picture, choose one with a happy, approachable expression. The goal is to network and grow connections. Unless you have a reason to choose a different facial expression, it has been my experience that social and approachable works best on LinkedIn.

Often, I get asked, "What should I wear in my profile picture?" The answer is you should wear what you would wear to work. Select an outfit that is appropriate at your office or in your industry. For example, a lawyer may need to wear a suit, but an IT professional may want to wear a graphic t-shirt.

Positive Samples:

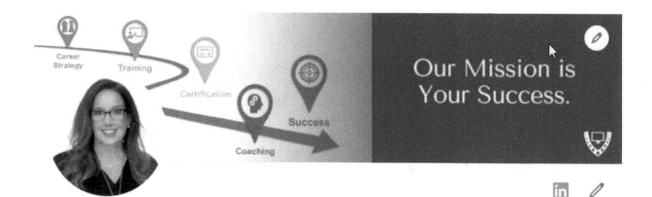

CREATING A MEMORABLE HEADLINE

Your headline consists of the 1–4 lines underneath your name. It is your opportunity to tell the world what your passion is. If you are employed, then the headline is an opportunity to reinforce your brand. If you are job searching, you will want to use the job titles you are searching for and keywords related to your target occupation.

Tip: If you are job searching, please see the workbook *Finding the Jobs I Want* by Suzanne Ricci for specific information on using LinkedIn for Job Searching.

When creating headlines for career success, I like to use vertical bars (|) to separate phrases or words, but you can use commas, forward slashes, or emojis if appropriate for your brand or industry. It is also ok to write in the first person on LinkedIn.

Examples:

Cybersecurity Analyst | Security+, ITIL | Certified Ethical Hacker | Splunk | Penetration Testing

I coach HR Professionals to become Business Leaders who work in the People space | I consult and help reinvent HR & Leadership Teams, Process & Culture | HR Expert & Strategist | CHRO | CPO

IT Certification Expert | Guide to 1000s of IT & Business Professionals Looking for Career Success | Author | Techie | "Talent Acquisition Talks" Podcast Host | COVID-19 Hero of Tampa Bay | Tampa Bay Tech "Bridge Builder"

BACKGROUND PHOTOS

You always hear that a picture is worth 1000 words. Your LinkedIn Background photo is no different. I like to think of it as my personal billboard, which displays my brand. People almost always look at graphics, but they don't always read. Truthfully, studies show people read 20% of what is on a page. Let your graphic showcase your brand. For career success, you can use this photo to showcase:

• A visual interpretation of your branding statement.

• Upcoming events you are marketing.

• Your small business.

• A trait associated with your brand.

Sample: Joel Morales – Joel is a cloud architect. Joel is displaying all of his certifications on top of the skyline where he lives. This shows confidence in his abilities and his love for his community. This is an example of his branding statement.

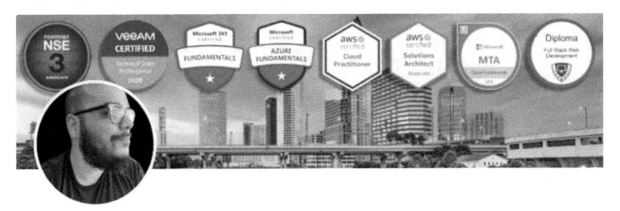

Sample: Kasandra Perez – Kasandra is a career strategist using her background photo to show off an upcoming course.

Sample: Dominick Ray – Dominick's background graphic displays his company. He is a photographer who uses LinkedIn to market his business heavily.

Sample: Barbara Gomez - Barbara is in HR. She is a positive person, and her background graphic reinforces this trait.

The above are four excellent examples of LinkedIn profile pages using their background photos to really show off their brands.

There are a few things to avoid when choosing a background photo.

- Plain landscape photos (i.e., beaches, gardens, rolling hills, etc.)

- Skylines by themselves, especially if it isn't your city.

- Pictures that don't represent your brand.

- Blurry or pixelated photos.

Canva is an online graphics tool (www.canva.com), which currently has a free version. They also have LinkedIn background photo templates you can use, customize, and make your own.

THE ABOUT SECTION

The about section in LinkedIn is the place to tell your story. Answer the statement "Now, tell me about yourself." You have a 2000-character limit and should write in the first person, using I. You want to start strong when writing your "about" section. In the book Adweek Copywriting *Handbook,* the author writes about the slippery slope of writing. Your "about me" should follow the same format. Your first sentence should be so impactful and grabbing that I read the second, then the third, then the fourth, and so on. Before I know it, I am at the bottom, and I have read your entire about section.

The reason to start strong with something impactful is that the about section will often get cut off, and a "see more" button will appear. You need to give someone a reason to click on the "see more."

On LinkedIn, the desktop version will show the first three lines of your "about" section. On mobile, only the first 25–30 characters will show.

When writing your "about" section, make it keyword-rich for your industry and job title. Adding keywords will help you come up in more search results. Also, consider adding some bullets. Bullets are more accessible for individuals to scan or read.

I always like to include a skills list at the bottom of an "about" section. It allows you to add in more keywords, and if someone is going to scan, it is easy to browse.

My final tip for the "about" section is to add a call to action. Tell someone to contact you or email you if you are comfortable doing so.

SAMPLE LINKEDIN ABOUT SECTION

I have a relentless drive to win. Because of this drive, I learned to create and follow well-planned recipes for success in everything I set my mind to. Recognizing my abilities and the happiness I find in helping others, I started sharing the strategies I employ in my own life via well-crafted career success plans.

- I offer career advice based on experience and individual training plans designed for my clients' goals.

- I create staff education programs that are goal-oriented and align with a company's mission.

- I have helped thousands of others find their way to where they want to be.

- I take great pleasure in assisting others to reach their full potential.

- I believe "if you want to lead, you have to read."

- I strive to read more than thirty books per year on success and life-improvement.

Don't hesitate to reach out to me and share a great read or write up a success tip you feel needs to be shared. I love learning!

If you need career coaching or career guidance, reach out.

Email: suzanne@computercoach.com

Twitter: @SuzanneRicci

Linkedin:www.linkedin.com/in/SuzanneRicci

Skills: Adobe Photoshop, Illustrator, HTML / CSS / Javascript, Content Writing, Microsoft Word, Excel, PowerPoint, Outlook, Access

FEATURED MEDIA

On LinkedIn, individuals can use the featured media section. The featured media section is below your "about" section and allows you to showcase "social proof" of your skills and achievements. This is a great place to show off the work you have done. It can contribute to your career success. Some things you can show off in this section include:

- Articles

- LinkedIn posts

- External blogs

- Graphics or projects

- Videos

- and more

I recommend taking advantage of the feature media section because it allows you to add colorful visuals to your profile page that can help you stand out.

OTHER LINKEDIN CAREER SUCCESS TIPS

- Join groups and share information with like-minded individuals.

- Ask for recommendations.

- Personalize your LinkedIn URL.

- Add fifty relevant skills to your skills section.

BE EXCITING, AND BE ENGAGING

One of the greatest opportunities LinkedIn presents for individuals engaging in career success strategies is the ability to share relevant information, create content, and stand out in your community.

Post at least one time per day; engage; and comment on other posts that are in line with your interests, job titles, and industries. You can automate your postings using a tool that integrates with LinkedIn (like HootSuite or LinkedIn Helper).

OUT-OF-THE-BOX THINKING

LinkedIn is a powerful tool that can be used to help you move toward your defined career success. Finally, here are three additional strategies you can start using today to get people who aren't in your network to notice you.

1. Strategically comment on the posts of second or third connections. We get notified when someone in our network engages with a post. Start taking the opportunity to write comments that allow for conversations with the author or others. People are sure to read your comment, wonder who you are, and start sending you connection requests.

2. We all have people in our network with large numbers of connections. Strategically ask these people questions or engage with them using the @Mention. Everyone likes to get noticed. Using this technique, you can come up in the news feed of their connections.

3.   On LinkedIn, you can follow hashtags. Content that uses the hashtags you follow may come up in your newsfeed, regardless if you are connected to the author. Using relevant hashtags on your posts can help your posts come up in newsfeeds of those you aren't (yet) connected with. Using five hashtags or less per post is considered ideal.

Start using these tips, so you can stand out and get more eyes on your LinkedIn profiles, more connection requests, and more opportunities.

CHAPTER 6

BUILDING LEADERSHIP SKILLS

Some people are natural-born leaders. The rest of us? Well . . . we need to work on it, and to become a good leader requires you to work on it *daily*. It's impossible to become a great leader in a day. But it is possible to learn the traits of a good leader. John C. Maxwell, a premier author and speaker in the field of leadership development, writes and speaks of a concept he calls "The Law of the Lid." Basically, the lid is your leadership potential. If you have low leadership skills, then you will hit the lid and not grow, thus restricting your ability. If you have high leadership skills, then the lid is high and thus allows you to become more successful before hitting your max.

Most leadership experts agree you can develop leadership skills. Personally, I wasn't one of the few that was born a natural leader. I am, like most of us, the one that has to work on my leadership ability every day.

I often say, "if you want to lead, you have to read." I am an avid reader of personal development literature. I don't generally read novels. All of my readings are books that help me grow as an individual. I read books on leadership, management, success stories, concepts, sales strategies, and more. I have to admit . . . I don't finish every book I start . . . GASP . . . If I get to a point where I feel it's repetitive, not applicable, or boring, I move on with no shame. My time is limited (as is everyone's), and I want to make sure I get the best ROI I can. I strive to read a book each week. That means fifty-two books per year. Sometimes I make it; sometimes, I don't. However, it's been years since I have gotten to December 31st and felt unaccomplished in my book reading. Reading is an important way to add on leadership skills.

1. Practice, practice, practice. I put into motion the things I read about that I think will help me be better at leadership, sales, management, whatever. I *try* them. My rule of thumb is at least thirty days. Sometimes, thirty days doesn't make sense, so you have to use some common sense with the application of the material. After my assessment period is over, I evaluate and make a decision based on my experience. Did the tactic or strategy work? Based on my experience, can I make it better? Can I tweak it?

2. Don't beat yourself up—ever! If you go for a stretch not applying/reading or you realize the tactic or strategy you tried is or was a big mistake, don't dwell on it. Change your ways and move forward. If you look back, you'll fall back. I consulted for a company, and the president once quoted Denzel Washington's commencement quote at the University of Pennsylvania: "If you're going to fall, try and fall forward." When I first heard this, I thought to myself, how do you fall forward? Well, the answer is by minimizing the impact. If you try a leadership technique and it starts to make sales decline or you're getting strange vibes from others, then go back immediately to the prior tactic. If the prior tactic isn't the one you want to stick with, then use it while you regroup.

Leadership development is important for career and life success. Whatever or however many leadership skills you decide you want to develop, be sure you add some kind of leadership development to your annual upskilling list. Below are some quick tips I have found to help in getting started adding leadership skills.

- Sign up for motivational quotes

- Commit to reading fifteen minutes a day about success strategies, leadership, etc. Everyone has an extra fifteen minutes for development.

- Sign up for leadership development classes.

Tip: Don't forget audiobooks are a great way to fill commute times. I listen to audiobooks while I'm by myself. This can be when I am walking, cleaning the house, driving, etc.

STAY FOCUSED

Even if developing your leadership qualities doesn't feel natural to you, don't underestimate the inherent skills you already possess. Think about the roles you play as a friend, a parent or coach, or maybe as a tutor. Identify your strengths and build on those characteristics. Any time you are in a position where you have more knowledge, expertise, or experience than someone else, you have the opportunity to be a leader. Don't hesitate to follow your instincts and natural abilities. Trust your own great ideas, and don't be afraid to be yourself.

Next, I'd like you to consider the role models, mentors, managers, teachers, and religious leaders you know, and think about which traits you'd most like to emulate—and which traits you'd prefer to avoid.

ACTIVITY

- Write down the traits of those you admire.

_____

- Write down the traits of those you would want to avoid.

_____

Use the positive and negative traits written down as your guide to creating a profile of yourself as the ideal leader.

- Check off the traits you already have and highlight the skills you need to learn.

- Look up resources to learn more about the traits you highlighted as needing to learn or improve.

When you are done with this exercise, you should have a pretty good roadmap to lead you on your leadership development journey.

And finally, before I send you on your way, I have one more piece of guidance. It may be a cliché, but actions really do speak louder than words. Great leaders know that their actions are what count the most. So, be impeccable with the examples you set for others. And next time you get that group assignment, instead of doing all the work, you'll be ready to step in and lead instead.

ACTIVITIES

- What books have you read within the last ninety days?

  _____

- What magazines do you subscribe to?

  _____

- Do you have any blogs you read regularly? List them.

  _____

- What podcasts do you enjoy?

  _____

Leadership skills are crucial to career success, and developing leadership skills can help you fast-track your career to the top. While technical skills and a college degree are always important, to be an effective leader, you should have some soft skills such as the ability to listen attentively and communicate clearly, among others.

Developing *critical* thinking skills, learning how to motivate and empower those around you, increasing your discipline, and getting out of your comfort zone are some other important steps to enhancing your leadership traits. You must also continually challenge yourself to improve your leadership capabilities.

Having a steady track record of being successful in leadership roles in your professional and personal life gets you where you want to go: whether it's a new job or a higher position.

When we discuss leadership, it is important to remember there are leadership opportunities all around us. Leadership isn't just a business skill. We can display leadership in our personal lives as well.

Here are nine actions you can take to develop leadership skills

1. **Be a Critical Thinker:** Good leaders are critical thinkers. This means they can think ahead, anticipate events or issues before they occur, and take action to help their team manage these issues. Thus, as a leader, you should foresee potential problems, develop strategies to prevent or mitigate these problems, and be aware of potential opportunities to benefit your team and company. When an employee calls your attention to a problem, you should help them determine the cause and adopt preventive measures to ensure it doesn't negatively impact the company and the customers.

2. **Don't Be Complacent:** If you want to be a good leader, you shouldn't be afraid to move out of your comfort zones or, more directly, learn competencies or skills that fall outside your primary knowledge area. Undertake more responsibilities, as this will enable you to learn more and eventually place you in a leadership position in your workplace. Also, others will easily accept you as a leader because you would have established a track record of taking the initiative, being a student of learning, and utilizing that newfound knowledge for making improvements.

3. **Listen Effectively:** To be an effective leader, you need communication skills –whether it's presenting in front of the team, developing and writing a business strategy, or communicating to employees and clients. One of the essential communication skills for a leader is listening. If you aren't a good listener, you'll be unable to get feedback from others and get a sense of what team members think about a project. To listen effectively, you need to maintain eye contact, respond appropriately and avoid distractions. Remember that communication is not just about verbal communication; pay attention to body language and gestures to determine what people are saying.

4. **Motivate Others:** A true leader should be able to energize and motivate others who have lost their ambition or passion. How can you motivate people? First, you must be aware of the needs and wants of those involved. Sometimes, people lose their motivation because they are facing certain challenges. They may be tired of doing the same tasks over and over or are disappointed they are not being asked to get involved. A good leader frequently seeks out team members to see how they're doing, listens attentively, and empowers them to be more involved in the process.

5. **Be Disciplined:** Discipline is required to execute any goal, whether personal or professional. For instance, let's say you and your team members want to create a new product to attract investors. The new product offers many benefits and could be the next big thing in the market. However, without discipline, the team might not work in synergy to get the best result. This is why to be a great leader, you need to be self-disciplined and ensure others on your team are also.

6. **Continuous Learning:** As former US president John F. Kennedy rightly said, "Leadership and learning are indispensable to each other." When your environment is changing rapidly, it is crucial to constantly learn and challenge yourself. Learn from other leaders; study their qualities, mannerisms, and methods of communication; and incorporate some of their traits into your style, engaging in upskilling opportunities specifically for soft skills and leadership.

7. **Know How to Delegate:** "The best executive is the one who has sense enough to pick good men to do what he wants done and self-restraint to keep from meddling with

them while they do it," said Theodore Roosevelt. A successful leader doesn't micromanage; instead, he or she delegates tasks to employees. Delegating roles will allow you to concentrate on your personal goals while enabling employees to feel more involved and develop new skills. As a project leader, most of the blame or accolades for the work go to you in the end. Thus, it is important that you oversee the project, delegating tasks to those who have the skills to accomplish them. Ensuring clarity of roles, responsibilities, and deadlines is crucial to delegation and getting a project completed. I always remind myself to "believe but verify." Keep this in mind when you are delegating. You still need to follow up and ensure the tasks are done and done right.

8. **Handle Conflicts:** Conflicts are inevitable in the workplace. Being able to handle difficult people and resolve conflict amounts to solid leadership. A good leader should be able to step up and talk to employees who don't work to the best of their abilities and bring negative attitudes to work. However, handling conflicts should always be done privately. Leaders need to be honest and straightforward. This requires a great deal of courage, as it isn't easy to point out a problem or fire someone.

9. **Be a Follower:** If you want to be a good leader, you should learn to acknowledge the value of your team, encourage them to learn from each other, and take time to interact with them and know them better. Don't be quick to dismiss an idea regardless of how it sounds; instead, show interest, and help its creator determine if it a good idea. Believe in them, and assist them in stepping out of their comfort zones. Recognize and encourage others to take the type of initiative you took when you were just starting, building your skillset and honing your leadership skills.

Developing leadership skills plays a huge role in career advancement and enables you to impact people around you. If you want to become a leader, take the actions outlined above seriously. If you already are a leader, identify areas that need improvement and adopt the necessary skills.

CHAPTER 7

HOW FAILURE CAN LEAD TO CAREER SUCCESS

Many people ask if it is possible for failure to help achieve career success. If you are one of those who doubt that experiencing failure can help you achieve success, that's okay, but the truth is that it is possible to turn your failures into life lessons that can help you achieve career success. It's important to remember, failure is temporary; although I recognize some failures can seem forever, they really aren't.

When you fail, there is always a lesson to learn from the experience. To become successful in your career, you need to critically analyze your failures and map out the key ways to prevent a reoccurrence. So, in short . . . you need to learn from them.

Still, sounds vague? Keep reading as I walk you through the detailed steps to turn your failure into career success.

WHAT IS CAREER SUCCESS?

Remember, the definition of career success varies. This is because everyone has a different vision of what they want to achieve in their career. We talked about this a lot in chapters 1–3. Perhaps your definition of career success is staying in an organization long enough to attain a great height as an executive, switching companies to know how they function and getting an idea of what it takes to run a business in the future, or just making an impact on the organization for which you work. No matter what your definition of career success is, it is possible to learn a lot from your previous experience . . . including your failures.

HOW TO TURN FAILURE INTO CAREER SUCCESS

After defining what career success means to you, you must take a moment to face your failure. Start by following these steps:

ACTIVITY

- List out areas you have failed. First, ask yourself some critical questions like, in what areas have I failed?

  _____

- If I ignore these areas, what will be the repercussion?

  _____

- Will these failures prevent me from climbing the career ladder at my present company?

  _____

List out the event leading up to the failure:

- What were the events that led to your failure?

  _____

- How did you react to the situation?

  _____

  o   Was it self-doubt? Or lack of information to handle the situation?

  _____

Clearly point out the lesson learned:

- Start from the events leading up to the failure, and pick lessons learned.

  _____

- How are you going to do better?

  _____

- Are you going to ask questions, seek opinions, increase your professional network, etc.?

  _____

Facing your failure and finding out why you had specific outcomes can prevent it from reoccurring in the future. In addition, you will be able to make decisions and take actions that bring about favorable results. For example, you may find specific skills you need to enhance or soft skills you need to further develop to not fail again.

SOME LESSONS YOU CAN LEARN FROM FAILURE

- **Failure gets you out of a routine:** Perhaps you just got a new job and you've set up a daily routine. You go to work, fulfill your responsibilities, and head home immediately when the clock strikes 5 p.m. However, on a certain day, the company gets a business deal, which means you need to work late in the evening—impossible, given your current schedule. Since you can't attend to this client, he opts for a new company. The management gets wind of what you've done; you get queried and suspended but luckily, not fired. What do you think this failure will do to you? Of course, you'll learn that routines do not work when it comes to a corporate environment. Hopefully, you will learn you need to be willing to go above and beyond for the company if you wish to rise to the management level. You'll learn that clients/customers are the business's lifelines, and you need to ensure you're always available to address their needs and answer their questions. The bottom line is, you'll get out of the routine and become more creative at your workplace. This failure can help you learn the above and, next time, not repeat the same actions.

- **Failure makes you consider new opportunities:** Let's say you get a job as a marketing officer, and you've been trying to get new customers, but you're not successful. You can start analyzing your strengths and weaknesses. Do you have poor communication skills, or is this role not meant for you? You may begin to introspect your motives in accepting the role at all. Was it to get by, or are you passionate about marketing? If it was only to have a source of income, you could start considering new job opportunities. Rather than going down the rabbit hole, consider jobs that will allow you to apply your true strengths. Find out the skills you should learn for the role, and start applying for available positions. But if you are passionate about marketing, get the necessary training to sharpen your skills that will make you better at your craft.

- **Failure teaches you about change:** Change remains constant. If you are someone that finds change hard to accept, you might find yourself struggling. When you experience failure, specifically in your career, you might recognize the need to change. There could be something you are doing that is not working, and you might need to overhaul the process and replace it. Failure tells you to consider other ways to achieve a goal. And then, you'll start thinking of things you can change to help your career progression. For example, do you find it hard working with colleagues? You may not be a good team player. Or maybe you prefer working independently. Having a situation, like a failure, gives you the ability to think. Thinking brings new ideas. And one of these ideas could help your career success.

- **Failure keeps you humble:** As a human, when everything goes well, you may see yourself as untouchable. However, when failure comes crashing down, it might seem like the end of the world. The truth is that most successful people in the world today are humble. They have gone through a series of failures and realized that anything could happen at any point in time. If your head is way too high in the clouds, falling could be incredibly painful.

At the very least, failure will teach you that you don't have it all figured out.

No doubt, failure could lead to career success. However, to grow past your previous experience, you must see failure as a learning opportunity to become a better professional. Take time to analyze areas you have failed in the past and draw a map of important lessons learned.

CHAPTER 8

FINDING AND KEEPING MENTORS

For career success, having a mentor is essential. These are people who make the journey to a successful career easier. They prevent you from falling into loops you wouldn't have otherwise noticed, and they show you the ropes, so you don't have to spend time going around in circles. When you have a mentor, it implies that there is someone to talk to when things are not going so well.

The question I get asked a lot is where to find a mentor and how to keep one. In this chapter, I'll address exactly that.

WHO IS A MENTOR?

A mentor is an experienced individual, a professional in their field, who guides a less experienced individual, or a "newbie," in their professional journey. A mentor imparts knowledge, wisdom, and expertise to a less experienced individual, the mentee.

For this relationship to succeed, the mentor has to genuinely have the mentee's best interest in mind. This will show through:

- Providing the necessary resources the mentee may need in their career.

- Giving actionable advice whenever the need arises.

- Providing an insider's perspective.

- Introducing critical contacts in the industry to help the mentee's professional journey.

HOW TO FIND A MENTOR

I think it's important to point out that you can have formal or informal mentors. For me, an informal mentor is someone who gives you advice and someone you feel comfortable asking their opinion but you never formalize a mentor/mentee relationship. Regardless of the relationship, below are a few points to help you find a mentor.

Have a plan: Before finding a mentor, you need to plan what that relationship will look like or what you would like to get out of the relationship. When you have a solid career plan, which we discussed in the first few chapters, it becomes easier to identify how mentors can help you.

ACTIVITIES

What do you want to get out of a mentor relationship?

_____

Examples include: career guidance, skill gap identification, and introductions.

1.

2.

3.

4.

5.

Tip: You need to be a person of value. Many mentors are looking for talented people to impart their knowledge. You have to be competent, teachable, enthusiastic, and reliable to attract these mentors.

When you perform well at your workplace and are eager to go above and beyond to ensure company growth, it won't be long before people are interested in mentoring you. Even if they don't come to you, they'll be thrilled when you go to them.

ACTIVITY

Look around your professional circle. Are there successful colleagues you admire? List them:

1.

2.

3.

4.

5.

Are you comfortable with these people? Your mentor should be someone you share the same values with to prevent frequent opposing views, leading to a bad relationship.

Yes, I am comfortable ___

No, I am not comfortable ___

THINGS TO KNOW WHEN FINDING A MENTOR

- **A mentor can be anyone:** Mentors don't have to be people in your profession. Mentors can be family members, friends, teachers, etc. It should be someone whose work ethic and personal achievements you admire. As a career person, having someone who knows the intricacies of your organization or industry is better.

- **Get a well-informed mentor:** A mentor must be knowledgeable and well informed. He or she should know about skills, training, and certifications that can advance your career. An ideal mentor can recommend key people that will help you climb the career ladder.

- **Strengthen an existing relationship:** When reaching out to a prospective mentor, don't be too direct in asking for mentorship. Some people will say right away, "Will you be my mentor?" That sounds predatory and could put off the prospect. If you're already in communication with someone you feel could be a good mentor, all you need do is strengthen the relationship. Finding a mentor is a process. You have to approach the person casually and gradually. Mentoring relationships can be developed by following up.

- **Have multiple mentors:** You can have more than one mentor. Having numerous mentors means you have different options when seeking advice concerning your career. Moreover, if one mentor is unavailable, you can always call up another. That way, you are not stuck on issues that you need urgent answers to.

HOW TO KEEP A MENTOR

Finding a mentor isn't enough; you need to take the proper steps to ensure they remain your mentor for a long time.

Mentors have their own lives, too, so don't expect them to be available at all times. Find out times they'll be free for a meetup. It could be monthly, quarterly, or yearly. It depends on how much time they are ready to invest in you. For a mentor to invest time in you, you will have to be valuable too.

Tip: No one likes to keep giving without getting anything in return.

Human relationships depend on a give and take flow. It's not different from a mentor and mentee relationship. While a mentor might not necessarily require much from you, it's reasonable to offer your help with something they are struggling with within your expertise.

If you have a meeting with your mentor, be there at the appropriate time—or better yet, be early. Please don't keep them waiting. That will show you don't value their time or sacrifices. If you have to adjust your schedule to make a meeting possible, do it. You're the one gaining.

You'll need to have the emotional intelligence to build a long-term relationship with your mentor. Know how to manage disagreement on issues, and avoid arguments that question his or her expertise.

Ask questions politely, and don't stop being appreciative.

FINAL THOUGHTS ON KEEPING MENTORS

Finding and keeping a mentor shouldn't be difficult if you know the height you wish to attain in your career. But you have to be ready to deal with the responsibilities that come with having a mentor, including showing up. You also need to be proactive. If you are receiving advice about getting specific certification or training, make sure you act on the advice. This way, the mentor will see you are serious about scaling up your career, making them more eager to help you out. Above all, be appreciative of the time that the mentor spends with you.

CHAPTER 9

DEVELOPING RESILIENCE FOR CAREER SUCCESS

According to the American Psychological Association, resilience is the process of adapting well in the face of adversity, trauma, tragedy, threats, or even significant sources of stress.

In simple terms, we describe resilience as the ability to get back on your feet when something goes wrong instead of cracking under pressure.

Resilience is a trait that can break or make your career. Fostering career resilience allows you to adapt to changes in the workplace, including mergers, acquisitions, reengineering, downsizing, furloughing, and so on.

The current workforce environment has made resilience a must-have characteristic for employees, as pressure and stress continue to take a toll on individuals. The good news is that everyone has some resilience. Maybe the quantity varies, but everyone has some. The better news is that it can be learned, and much like a muscle, the skill can be honed and perfected when "exercised."

In this section, we will explore the various ways career resilience can be developed, but first, let's understand the concept of career resilience a little better.

WHAT IS CAREER RESILIENCE?

As we discussed, according to experts, career resilience is the ability to adapt to changing career circumstances, even when the circumstances are discouraging or disruptive. It involves navigating all the inevitable bumps; ups and downs; and twists and turns on your career path.

Career resilience is necessitated by the nature of today's workplace environment: uncertain, complex, volatile, and ambiguous. Because many scenarios could threaten to derail your career, this skill is no longer a "nice to have" but a core professional competency.

HOW CAN YOU DEVELOP CAREER RESILIENCE?

1. **Build an effective network:** Building an effective network is fundamental to developing career resilience, as it can help you avoid potentially difficult career events. It entails growing your existing network and establishing new connections with like-minded individuals in your industry and beyond. Adam Grant, a professor at The Wharton School and author of *Give and Take,* talks about how giving your time and energy to people you care about is the best way to build your network. Keep in mind that networks are not built on a transactional basis but, rather, on goodwill and paying it forward. Most importantly, one must focus on building relationships, not contacts. Also, don't wait until there's trouble to start fostering relationships; start today.

2. **Manage your career like a business:** Managing your career like your own business (Ruth Smith Inc.) allows you to think like an entrepreneur, constantly looking for ways to improve your personal brand. Your brand is the collection of skills and experiences that make you unique; it is how you present yourself to the world. To stand out from the crowd and capture the interests of clients and employers, ensure you clearly communicate who you are and what you do.

3. **Embrace lifelong learning:** Continuous learning is another key ingredient for building career resilience. Stay up to date on the latest technology and new trends; take online courses; and attend industry conferences, seminars, and workshops. Take charge of your development, and cultivate your skills. Remember, no amount of knowledge is too much knowledge. Anything you can do to develop your skills and expertise will help to increase your self-confidence and, ultimately, your resiliency.

4. **Become Positive:** Positive people are more resilient than pessimists. If your mind continually focuses on the negative, don't worry; you can work to become more optimistic. You can begin by becoming very self-aware. Start by thinking less about what goes wrong, and start focusing more on what goes right. Keeping a journal may help. If you notice you keep worrying about the same things, write those thoughts down and commit to learning how you can eliminate those worries. Keep a record of the good things in your life and your achievements—regardless of their "size." At the end of every day, write a few lines about what is great and what you're most really grateful for in your current situation. In addition, you may want to consider writing out and reading affirmations over and over.

5. **Forgive and let go:** Unfortunately, we are often our own harshest critics, especially in retrospect. Make peace with the fact there will always be things you didn't know . . . until you came to know them. I often say, "We don't know what we don't know." Harboring resentment, whether directed at yourself or others, only achieves one thing: keeping you stuck. Forgiveness is a crucial step in moving forward and in building resilience.

6. **Look at setbacks as opportunities:** Learn to see and harness the potential opportunity in an adverse situation. Remember, it's not what happens to you that matters; it's how you handle it.

7. **If you get laid off, use that opportunity to go back to school and upskill:** Persevere; don't settle for less; all you need is within your reach if you keep pushing. Remember this: the most successful people in the world are also the most resilient. J.K. Rowling's

first Harry Potter manuscript was rejected by twelve leading publishers before being accepted. The famous Walt Disney was fired from the Kansas City Star because his editor felt he "lacked imagination and had no good ideas." Sir James Dyson (who, by the way, doesn't have an engineering degree) went through 5,126 failed prototypes over the course of fifteen years before developing the best-selling bagless vacuum cleaner that led to a net worth of $5.4 billion.

The next time you hit a career brick wall, think back to when you were able to persevere. Recreate the steps you took at that time.

PHYSICAL HEALTH

Get in shape. You might not hear or read this often, but your career is influenced by everything you do to stay in shape—physically, emotionally, and spiritually. Managing your fitness, energy level, and time will help you do your best work and build the resilience that will keep you going in tough times. I try to walk at least one mile every day. It makes a world of difference.

Keep in mind that your career can't soar when you're neglecting the rest of your life. Write a brief personal vision statement, create a list, or draw a diagram touching on your most essential values and the key parts of your life. Even when you're battling with a career crisis, you will feel better if you can keep your perspective.

Lastly, look at the big picture. Have an overall career plan, as we discussed in the first few chapters. This will help you stay on course if something does go wrong. Focusing day to day or week to week may seem daunting, but when you look at your career five years from now, success might look very different.

FINAL THOUGHTS ON RESILIENCE

Resilience is crucial to every aspect of your life, your career included. The trait can be cultivated and nurtured and has become an indispensable competency in today's challenging business landscape. Being optimistic, embracing lifelong learning, building robust relationship networks, getting in shape, and forgiving are instrumental in developing career resilience.

Career success is ongoing. Hopefully, the activities in this book will help

you continue to plan, execute, revise and move toward

your defined career success.

If you have any questions please feel free to

reach out to me at: Suzanne@ComputerCoach.com or

via LinkedIn at https://www.LinkedIn.com/In/SuzanneRicci

CPSIA information can be obtained
at www.ICGtesting.com
Printed in the USA
LVHW021622220922
728945LV00005B/406